REWILDING

BRINGING WILDLIFE BACK WHERE IT BELONGS

NEON SQUID

CONTENTS

WHAT IS REWILDING?

So, first things first, what does rewilding actually mean? Over the last few hundred years, human beings have had a huge impact on the world around us, and today there is much less nature around than there used to be. Rewilding projects are wildlife reintroductions that try to reverse that trend. They bring animals and plants back to areas from which they have disappeared—usually because we overhunted them or changed their habitat too much.

The plants and animals used in rewilding projects often come from groups kept in captivity. But biologists can also take animals from the wild and move them to other areas. This is called translocation.

TO REWILD OR NOT TO REWILD?

Scientists spend a lot of time trying to determine if a rewilding project is appropriate before they get started. They need to figure out why the species disappeared in the first place and then make sure those threats aren't a problem anymore. After all, if an animal was overhunted in the past, it is not okay to release that species back into the wild without making sure the same thing doesn't happen again.

Nobody does a reintroduction by themselves. Most projects involve many people, agencies, organizations, and universities all working together to help bring back the plants and animals that once disappeared from the wild.

A HOPEFUL FUTURE

There's a lot to be concerned about today if you care about the environment. The 20th century was full of sad stories of disappearing species and empty fields, forests, and oceans. But today you can find many people working hard to fix those mistakes and right those wrongs.

Turn the pages to read about incredible projects from all over the world and the unbelievable lengths to which people are willing to go. You might even be inspired to do your part to help your local wildlife!

THE JOURNEY OF THE
WHOOPING CRANES

Here's a common conundrum with rewilding projects: How do you teach animals raised in captivity to act like wild animals? This problem baffled scientists working to save whooping cranes—large wetland birds native to North America. By 1950, there were only 34 whooping cranes left in the wild, all members of a small population that migrated between Texas and Canada every year. After many years of being hunted, and because the prairies and marshes they needed to survive had been turned into farmland, the species was on the brink of extinction.

In the late 1960s, biologists decided it was time to try to step in. One injured Canadian crane joined 12 other cranes hatched from eggs that had been collected in the wild and raised in captivity. This group of captive birds eventually started producing babies that could be released back into the wild.

FOLLOW THE LEADER

Ultralight planes are small and a lot quieter than regular planes.

Some whooping cranes migrate long distances between the areas in the United States where they find food and spend the winter (Florida) and where they go to mate and raise chicks (Wisconsin). How would the crane chicks raised in captivity know where to go each year? To help them, biologists teamed up with ultralight plane pilots! The young birds were trained to fly with the planes, originally over small distances. Once the birds had gotten the hang of it, the pilots taught them the migration route used by their ancestors. It was a sight to see the plane soaring through the sky, followed by whooping cranes flying in formation. Unfortunately these efforts stopped in 2016 because only a few cranes produced babies on their own. This suggested they were not learning all of the life skills they needed.

ADOPTED PARENTS

With so few whooping cranes left in the wild, conservationists couldn't rely on just one strategy to work. Scientists hoped sandhill cranes (a closely related and relatively common species) could help raise whooping cranes and teach them how to be wild birds. In the 1970s and 1980s hundreds of whooping crane eggs were placed in sandhill crane nests for them to raise as their own. However, when these whooping cranes became adults they acted too much like their adopted parents and didn't socialize with other whooping cranes! Some even mated with sandhill cranes, creating hybrid babies known as whoophills.

Despite these failures, conservationists aren't giving up—they'll continue trying to save the whooping cranes.

DESPITE EFFORTS, THERE ARE STILL FEWER THAN 1,000 WHOOPING CRANES IN THE WILD.

A whooping crane chick in a sandhill crane nest.

THE TOADS THAT NEEDED A SHOWER

Amphibians such as frogs, toads, and salamanders are a group of animals at risk. Firstly, they are very sensitive to changes in their environment, because their slimy skin doesn't protect them like scales or fur can. Another reason they're in trouble is because they can be fussy creatures and often prefer specific habitats. This means some species can only be found in very small areas.

One example of an amphibian that ticks all of the above boxes is the Kihansi spray toad. This small amphibian only lives in Tanzania, in East Africa—but that's not all. Specifically it only lives among the rocks and plants sprayed by waterfall mist in the Kihansi Gorge!

In the late 20th century, a dam was built to help provide electricity to the residents of Tanzania. Although this project was important for people, it had unexpected effects on the Kihansi spray toad. Once the river was dammed there was much less water flowing over the gorge, which also meant there was much less mist for the shower-loving toads.

Suddenly, the special misty habitat was gone, and soon the Kihansi spray toad was too. Biologists believe they were extinct in the wild just a few years after the dam was finished.

Kihansi spray toads before the river was dammed.

A STICKY SITUATION

Fortunately, around 500 toads were collected from the wild right about the same time the dam was built. These toads went to the Bronx Zoo in New York City to start a breeding colony. Biologists wanted the captive toads to thrive and be healthy, but that was a challenge because of their special requirements. So the scientists created a water-spraying system that made the amphibians feel right at home. And it worked, because the toads were soon producing thousands of babies.

The Kihansi Dam was opened in 2000.

BACK TO THE GORGE

It wasn't long before there were enough Kihansi spray toads to release back into the wild. But there was a problem: The dam was still there. Without the wet and misty habitat the toads needed, there was no point in a reintroduction.

The scientists came up with a smart solution. They got engineers to create an artificial misting system! It used pipes and nozzles to spray water over the toad habitat that had dried up. In 2012, 2,000 toads were released back to their home under the gorge, and things seem to be going well. These toads may now have to rely on our help to survive in the wild, but so far, they've got it.

THE DAM BUILDERS

Beavers were hunted to extinction in England 400 years ago, partly so people could make warm and fashionable hats from their fur. And they remained absent until 2008... That year, several beavers were surprisingly observed in Devon, an area in the southwest of the country. Nobody knows exactly how they got there!

Although the unexpected comeback of the paddle-tailed rodents was celebrated by many, their reappearance was not without controversy.

Soon, evidence emerged that beavers weren't just living in Devon, but they were also building dams and lodges and making babies! Not everyone was happy about this. Local landowners and farmers were concerned about the beavers spreading diseases, so the government hatched a plan to remove them.

FLOOD PREVENTION

Meanwhile, scientists at the University of Exeter started researching the effects beavers were having on the environment. They revealed that beavers were actually bringing huge benefits to their new habitats. Their dams reduced flooding in the area, while also creating wetlands and meadows used by a wide variety of other species—including dippers, teals, water voles, and fish called brook lampreys. Because the beavers had proved their worth, the government reversed its decision and decided to let them stay.

Before the arrival of the beavers, flooding was common in the local villages.

KEYSTONE SPECIES

The important role that beavers play in ecosystems is why some call them a "keystone species." However, that's little consolation to some farmers, who are still concerned about how the changing waterways could affect their land. Fortunately, the government is eager to work with these farmers and figure out strategies that will benefit both people and beavers. Today, beavers are making themselves at home throughout Europe, despite once being in trouble just about everywhere. Thanks to conservation efforts and a growing appreciation for these creatures, there are now thought to be over a million across the continent.

BROOK LAMPREY

DIPPER

TEAL

WATER VOLE

RETURN OF
THE SCAVENGERS

When a California condor flies overhead it can take your breath away. With wingspans reaching nearly 10 ft (3 m), they cast gigantic shadows on the ground below. Although these big birds once flew throughout much of North America, by the 15th century they were already restricted to the west coast—and their range continued to shrink. By the mid-20th century, California condors were only nesting in the mountains along the southern California coast.

SCAVENGING PROBLEM

Condors are scavengers, which means they do not kill their own food. They find and eat things that are already dead, such as seals and whales that wash up on the shore. Sounds gross, but they love it! They also eat dead animals left behind by hunters—and this is a big problem if the hunters have used lead bullets, because lead can poison the birds. In fact, lead poisoning is considered one of the biggest threats to the species. By the 1980s, there were only about 20 California condors left. Eventually all of the remaining birds were captured and placed into captivity. They were extinct in the wild.

HAND PUPPETS

Several organizations and zoos teamed up to create a captive breeding colony of California condors. Their strategy relied on taking eggs from the birds, which often prompted the mothers to lay additional eggs. More eggs meant more condors. To make sure the babies knew how to behave like condors, biologists fed them using special hand puppets that looked just like the adult birds!

It's important condor chicks don't get used to being around humans.

SACRED ANIMALS

The first rewilding of California condors happened in 1992 in Baja California, Mexico. This was later followed by more reintroductions in California and Arizona. Today you might see a California condor if you visit those states, because there are now hundreds of the wild birds soaring through the skies again!

Another reintroduction is being organized by the Yurok Tribe of northern California. The California condor is a sacred bird to them, and they recognize the important role it plays in the ecosystem of their ancestral lands. They are working hard to bring the birds back to an area they have been missing from for 100 years.

The Yurok Tribe hope to release many California condors into the wild.

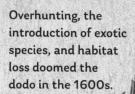
Overhunting, the introduction of exotic species, and habitat loss doomed the dodo in the 1600s.

WHY DO SPECIES DISAPPEAR?

Extinction can be a natural process. Over millions of years, many species have come and gone as the world has slowly changed. But today is different. In the modern world, species are not going extinct because of natural processes, but because of humans. Not only that, extinction is also happening much more rapidly now than at any time in the past. Most scientists would tell you that because we are responsible for these problems, we have a duty to reverse them. Wildlife populations are shrinking and disappearing for a few different reasons. Let's investigate some of the main problems.

CLIMATE CHANGE

In the near future, climate change—caused by humans burning fuels like coal and oil—will become a bigger problem for wildlife. Animals will have to adapt to changing temperatures, rising sea levels, and different weather patterns. Habitats will change, too. Some species that can easily move around, like birds, may try to find new places to live. Other species that can't leave so easily may have more trouble migrating. Animals that already live in the coldest places, like polar bears, might find that there is nowhere left for them to go.

HABITAT LOSS

Habitat loss can be obvious, like when a pond is turned into a parking lot, but it can be subtle too. For example, some forests rely on small wildfires every few years. Without these fires other species start to move in and crowd out the locals. When people start messing with these natural processes, the habitats can become less welcoming for the original plants and animals.

OVERHUNTING

Hunting too many animals used to be a big problem. It was responsible for crashing the populations of once very common species like bison and passenger pigeons. Today, we have lots of laws that limit how much hunting can take place. These rules can help make sure we do not make the same mistakes as our ancestors.

EXOTIC SPECIES

Today, a big threat to wildlife populations is the presence of non-native species. These animals get moved around by people (to be used as pets, for food, or by accident) and then escape or are released into the wild. These exotic creatures can have a big impact on the native species—by eating them, by competing with them for food, or by spreading diseases.

Escaped pet Burmese pythons are causing problems in Florida.

THE ANCIENT TORTOISES

The Galápagos Islands are a rocky archipelago off the west coast of Ecuador in South America. They're most famous for their incredible wildlife, an amazing collection of unique creatures that inspired naturalist Charles Darwin to come up with his theory of evolution after he visited the islands as a young man. Chief among the wonders of the Galápagos are giant tortoises—huge reptiles that can live to be over 100 years old!

These slow-moving beasts used to enjoy a peaceful life without any predators to worry about. That all changed in the 1800s. Whalers sailing the nearby seas realized tortoises tasted good and could be safely stored on ships for a long time. This was good news for sailors, but bad news for the Hood Island giant tortoise, a species found on one of the islands. The reptiles couldn't make enough babies to replace the adults taken as food, and their numbers shrank alarmingly.

HATCHING A PLAN

By the 1970s, there were only 15 Hood Island giant tortoises left—14 on Española Island and another at the San Diego Zoo in California. Scientists brought them all together at a breeding center on Santa Cruz Island. Safe and protected, they produced lots of babies over the years. The babies were then released back on Española Island. Some of these tortoises are now adults making their own babies—a very encouraging sign!

Under close supervision from scientists, the young tortoises had a much greater chance of reaching adulthood.

WILD CACTUS

A THORNY ISSUE

There is still work to do. Long ago, goats were introduced to the island, and they changed the vegetation, making less space for rare wild cactuses. These cactuses provide both food and shade for tortoises, and tortoises return the favor by eating them and pooping out their seeds to help spread the plants across the island. So scientists are working hard to increase the number of cactuses.

In 2020, after producing thousands of babies for the reintroduction program, all 15 original tortoises were released into the wild of Española Island. They've earned their retirement!

THE DESERT DWELLERS

Across rolling sand dunes and under a scorching sun, long-horned antelope called Arabian oryx used to make the deserts of the Middle East their home. However, thanks to hunting, they were nearly extinct by the end of the 20th century. Fortunately, scientists spotted the impending danger and formed a captive colony, hoping that they could use it to one day rewild the species. A handful of animals were captured from the wild and several more were donated from collections around the world. And just like that, there were nine Arabian oryx in captivity—with orders to make more. It worked! The oryx flourished and formed what is called the "World Herd," producing hundreds of babies over the years.

MIXED SUCCESS

Now it's great that babies were being born, but what would happen when they were taken home? Reintroductions took place in Oman, Saudi Arabia, Israel, the United Arab Emirates, and Jordan. Unfortunately it didn't all go according to plan.

In Oman, despite early promising signs, poaching and the loss of protected habitat has seen numbers of Arabian oryx once again decline. Meanwhile, in Saudi Arabia the animals suffered from diseases. As a result, many babies were separated from their parents and had to be hand-reared by people so they didn't get sick too. Luckily these oryx eventually started making babies of their own.

THE ARABIAN ORYX IS THE NATIONAL ANIMAL OF SEVERAL COUNTRIES IN THE MIDDLE EAST.

AGAINST THE ODDS

It hasn't always been easy, but as a result of conservationists' hard work, it is thought that more than 1,000 Arabian oryx now roam the deserts of the Middle East. And there are many more in captivity. All in all, it's thought to be one of the greatest success stories for a species once considered extinct in the wild.

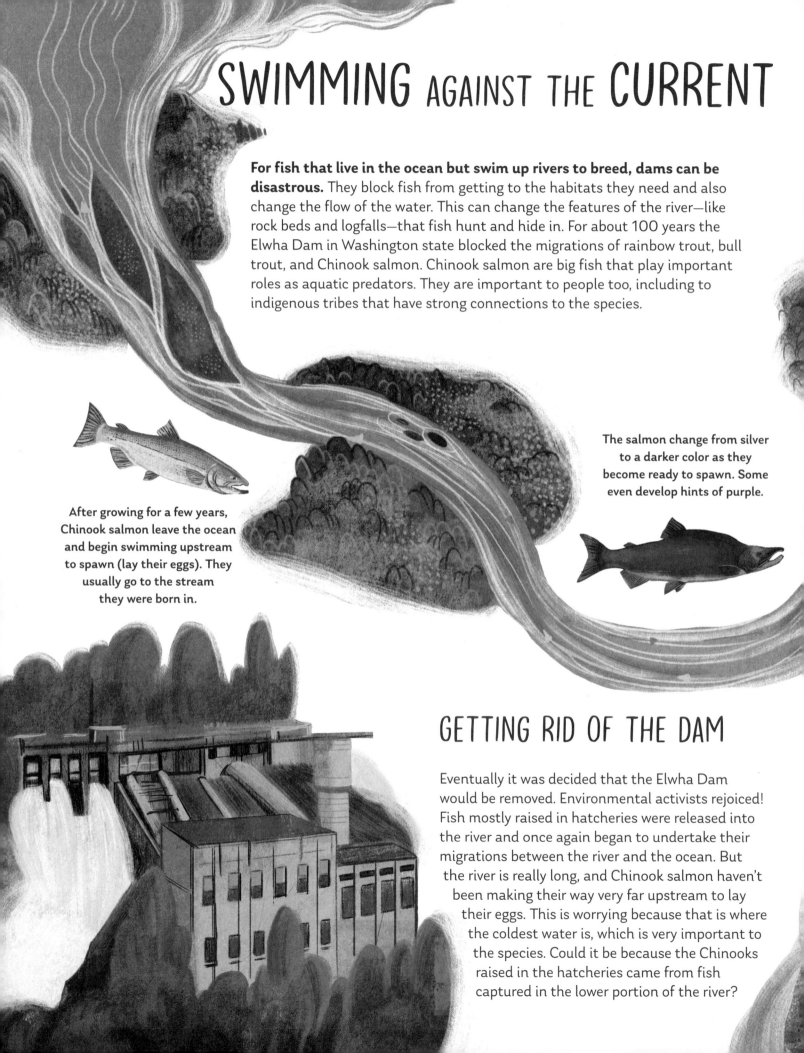

SWIMMING AGAINST THE CURRENT

For fish that live in the ocean but swim up rivers to breed, dams can be disastrous. They block fish from getting to the habitats they need and also change the flow of the water. This can change the features of the river—like rock beds and logfalls—that fish hunt and hide in. For about 100 years the Elwha Dam in Washington state blocked the migrations of rainbow trout, bull trout, and Chinook salmon. Chinook salmon are big fish that play important roles as aquatic predators. They are important to people too, including to indigenous tribes that have strong connections to the species.

The salmon change from silver to a darker color as they become ready to spawn. Some even develop hints of purple.

After growing for a few years, Chinook salmon leave the ocean and begin swimming upstream to spawn (lay their eggs). They usually go to the stream they were born in.

GETTING RID OF THE DAM

Eventually it was decided that the Elwha Dam would be removed. Environmental activists rejoiced! Fish mostly raised in hatcheries were released into the river and once again began to undertake their migrations between the river and the ocean. But the river is really long, and Chinook salmon haven't been making their way very far upstream to lay their eggs. This is worrying because that is where the coldest water is, which is very important to the species. Could it be because the Chinooks raised in the hatcheries came from fish captured in the lower portion of the river?

Salmon create gravelly pits in the stream floor where they lay their eggs. After spawning, all of the adult salmon die.

Chinook salmon eggs hatch in the spring, and the young fish (called fry) spend about five months in the stream.

Then the young fish make their way to the ocean, where they wait until it is their time to spawn!

THE NEXT GENERATION

Chinook salmon only have one chance in their lives to make babies, so they need to make the most of it. But there is good news: Many of the Chinook salmon are doing what they need to do and their babies are coming downstream to enter the ocean! Nevertheless everyone hopes they continue to increase in numbers, so that one day we will once again see hundreds of thousands of these fish making their way upstream to create the next generation.

RATTLESNAKE ISLAND

When there are few options left, islands can represent a good place to reintroduce wildlife where they won't be bothered by people.

What do you do if there is a species in need of help, but the public doesn't like that animal? Sometimes this rewilding issue arises with animals many believe to be dangerous, like snakes.

Timber rattlesnakes can be found throughout much of the eastern and central United States, but they're relatively rare in northern areas. This may be because it is colder and less suitable for the reptiles there. That said, they used to be much more common before humans decided they didn't want them around. And people haven't changed their minds—despite the species becoming increasingly rare.

Massachusetts only has five populations of timber rattlesnakes—you can count them all on one hand. That's not many when you consider they were probably once widespread throughout the state. Although reintroductions would benefit the species, there are sadly few people that want more snakes in their area.

IF NOT THERE, WHERE?

Government officials in Massachusetts thought they found a good solution for rewilding timber rattlesnakes. They planned to introduce 150 snakes to Mount Zion, a little-visited island in the Quabbin Reservoir, where they were unlikely to disturb people (and vice versa).

Unfortunately there was such an outcry about this plan from the locals that it was eventually canceled. As human populations grow, there are going to be fewer and fewer truly natural and isolated places. If these are the only places we're comfortable having wild animals, it will be very bad news for these species.

Timber rattlesnakes mostly eat small mammals, which often carry ticks and various diseases that can harm people.

CHARISMATIC CREATURES

If you know a friendly and charming person, you might think of them as charismatic. There are animals that people find charismatic too, and these tend to be large and cuddly-looking species, like tigers, bears, and wolves. Maybe we can relate to these creatures more than we can to, say, a timber rattlesnake, or a slug, or a wasp! Charismatic species tend to get a lot more attention than other species, which means there's more money and interest to support their rewilding projects.

Most people don't care about slugs. But these slimy creatures have an important role to play in our ecosystems: They chew up leaves, digest them, and return their nutrients to the soil.

Wasps are another unpopular group of species. Bees get a lot of credit for being important pollinators, but many wasps do this job too! And some wasps prey on insects that eat our crops.

THE TALKING PARROTS

Puerto Rico is an island in the Caribbean that used to be covered in beautiful forests. However, many of them were cut down by humans in the 20th century for timber and to make room for growing crops. This is called deforestation. This was bad news for the many species that lived on the island, like the Puerto Rico parrot (also known as the iguaca). Their population crashed with the decline of the forest, and by the 1970s there were fewer than 20 birds left, all within El Yunque National Forest.

Eggs and chicks were brought into captivity. Interestingly, because the captive flocks were formed from young birds, they were never taught how to sing and call by their actual parents. This meant they developed their own form of language! Some were probably influenced by the closely related Hispaniolan Amazon parrots, who were used as foster parents.

WATCHING CLOSELY

Because they speak a different language, there is some concern that the birds might struggle to communicate with other members of their species in the wild. When the birds were first released, researchers attached radio transmitters to the parrots so they could observe their behavior. That's how they learned that hawks were an important predator—they ate some of the released birds. Despite these setbacks, there are signs of hope. Today the species can be found in both El Yunque National Forest and Rio Abajo State Forest, though still in very low numbers.

A BREWING STORM

When populations of a species are low and animals are rare, ordinary problems become bigger problems. For example, in Puerto Rico there have always been hurricanes, but now, due to climate change, they are stronger and more frequent. If there were many thousands of birds, it wouldn't be a big deal if a few dozen or even a couple of hundred died during these violent storms. But because there aren't that many Puerto Rico parrots left in the wild, today hurricanes can be a major setback. The fate of the Puerto Rico parrots remains in the balance.

WHAT IS AN ECOSYSTEM?

Take a walk through a forest, in a field, or alongside sandy dunes. You'll see plants and hear insects; maybe a bird will fly overhead as you notice a turtle rustling around at your feet. They are all connected. Some species are found in many different places, while others are very picky about where they live, but either way they interact with the other species in their area. These interactions bind them together in what is called an ecosystem. When biologists reintroduce species to an area, they are putting a piece of an ecosystem back into place.

AFRICAN SAVANNA

The African savanna is one of the world's most famous ecosystems. It is unique because of its climate (warm temperatures and a rainy summer), its structure (vast grasslands and occasional acacia trees), and its species (from lions and zebras to vultures and meerkats). You will never see this exact combination of weather, plants, and animals anywhere else in the world. Even the smallest and seemingly most insignificant species are important members of their ecosystems, and when they are missing, the entire region is impacted.

GIVE ME SOME SPACE

When designing a rewilding project, it is important to think about its size. Biologists need to ensure that any animals reintroduced to an area have plenty of space to roam and grow. And it's important to remember that big animals will often need more space than smaller creatures! In the case of black-footed ferrets, biologists in the United States chose to rewild them in large ranches that contained a lot of prairie dogs to eat.

ECOSYSTEM ENGINEERS

Sometimes the goal of a reintroduction isn't just to benefit one species, but to repair an ecosystem. For example, wolves are common in many areas throughout the world, but if they disappear it means an important predator is missing. Bringing back wolves restores natural interactions between many species. The same is true for ecosystem engineers—animals that alter habitats in ways that benefit other species. For example, alligators use their bodies to dig depressions in the ground. These holes hold water even when swamps dry up and as a result are used by many other thirsty creatures.

THE WOLVES OF YELLOWSTONE

In Yellowstone National Park in Montana, one animal was top dog—the gray wolf.
For thousands of years packs of wolves roamed around, snacking on large mammals such as elk. They were what's known as an apex predator, a hunter at the top of the food web. At least they were... until humans got involved.

Predators play important roles in ecosystems, and when they are absent there can be ripple effects on other species. For example, when you lose a predator that eats plant-eating animals—herbivores—those prey animals might increase in numbers dramatically. In turn, the plants they rely on could become overgrazed, resulting in less overall food and a different-looking landscape.

HUNTED TO EXTINCTION

Wolves have been one of the most persecuted animals around the world, and many governments worked hard to wipe them out, even offering bounties. The United States was no exception, and even national parks offered wolves little protection. In the wild, wolves are fearsome opponents, with sharp teeth and the ability to work well as a team. But that didn't count for much in the face of guns. By around 1926, the last wolf had disappeared from Yellowstone National Park.

OVERRUN WITH ELK

Almost immediately, the elk population started increasing dramatically. Great numbers of elk started chomping on trees like aspen and cottonwood, whose roots helped stabilize stream banks used by fish like salmon. At the same time, coyote populations increased because the territorial wolves were no longer around to keep them in check. These coyotes started preying on pronghorn antelope fawns in greater numbers. It was clear that Yellowstone's ecosystem was out of whack!

In the second half of the 20th century, an increased appreciation for conservation set the stage for bringing wolves back to Yellowstone National Park.

THE WOLVES WERE
SEEN AS PESTS.
BUT THEY WERE
SOON MISSED.

BRINGING BACK
THE WOLVES

In 1995, 14 wolves from Alberta, Canada were captured and brought through the thick snow to Yellowstone. Wolves from this area were selected because it was similar to Yellowstone, with mountains, grassy meadows, and, most importantly, elk. These wolves already knew how to hunt the animals that would be present in their new home.

WELCOME TO YELLOWSTONE

The wolves spent the first couple of months in pens so they could get used to their surroundings, before they were released into the wild. The next year they were joined by 17 more wolves. The wolves formed packs, established territories, and settled in. And just like the scientists had hoped, the ecosystem started to recover.

Interestingly, after they were released some of the wolves learned how to take down bison, a much bigger—and potentially more dangerous—meal than elk. Today there are around 100 wolves in the park in approximately ten packs, although the numbers change somewhat over the years.

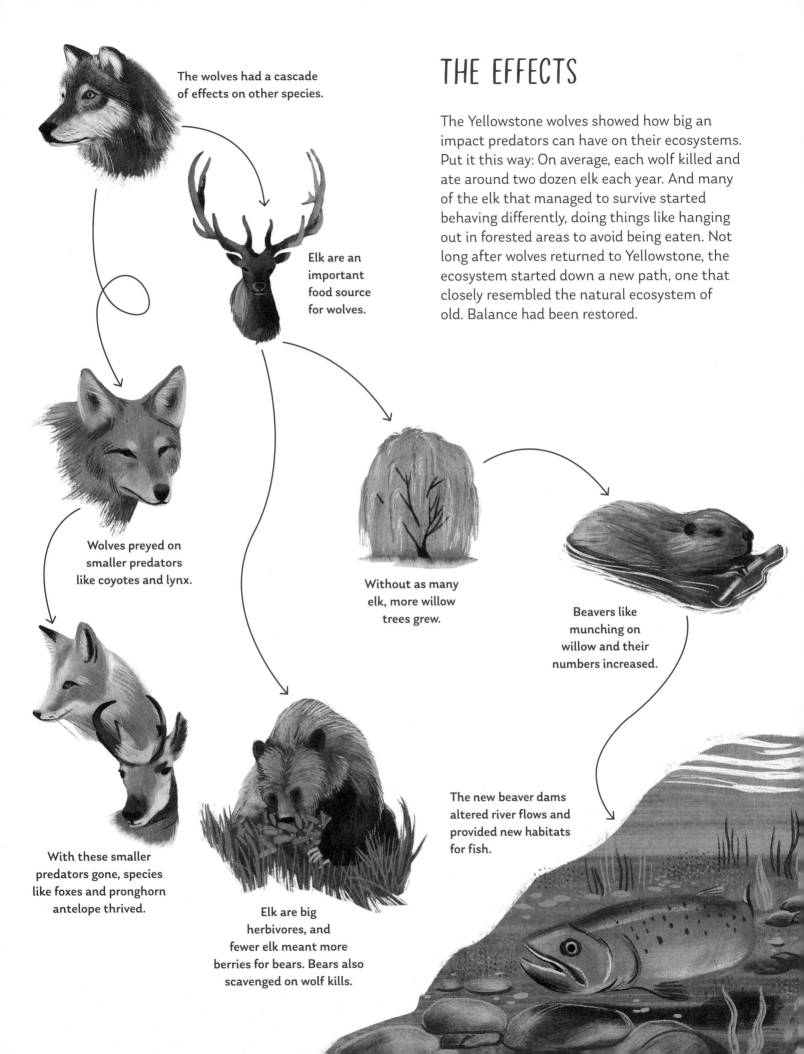

The wolves had a cascade of effects on other species.

THE EFFECTS

The Yellowstone wolves showed how big an impact predators can have on their ecosystems. Put it this way: On average, each wolf killed and ate around two dozen elk each year. And many of the elk that managed to survive started behaving differently, doing things like hanging out in forested areas to avoid being eaten. Not long after wolves returned to Yellowstone, the ecosystem started down a new path, one that closely resembled the natural ecosystem of old. Balance had been restored.

Elk are an important food source for wolves.

Wolves preyed on smaller predators like coyotes and lynx.

Without as many elk, more willow trees grew.

Beavers like munching on willow and their numbers increased.

With these smaller predators gone, species like foxes and pronghorn antelope thrived.

Elk are big herbivores, and fewer elk meant more berries for bears. Bears also scavenged on wolf kills.

The new beaver dams altered river flows and provided new habitats for fish.

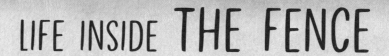

LIFE INSIDE THE FENCE

The Arid Recovery Reserve is located in a very dry and dusty region of southeastern Australia. For years this part of the country has been plagued by rabbits, cats, and foxes that were introduced from other countries. The cats and foxes happily feasted on the native wildlife, while the rabbits ate up the plants. This changed the landscape in ways that made it less hospitable for the native wildlife.

With little hope of getting rid of all of these invasive species for good, biologists, government agencies, and the Kokatha people (the indigenous people who live on the land) decided to build a large fenced-in reserve. Their aim was to remove all of the species that didn't belong there.

This approach allowed for the reintroduction of greater stick-nest rats, western barred bandicoots (both of which had been wiped out on mainland Australia and only existed on islands), greater bilbies, western quolls, and burrowing bettongs. The bettongs settled in the best—over a couple of decades 29 of these small marsupials released into the reserve turned into nearly 10,000!

FROM TOADS TO CAMELS, MANY INVASIVE SPECIES NOW LIVE IN AUSTRALIA.

WESTERN QUOLLS

GREATER BILBIES

WESTERN BARRED BANDICOOTS

Different kinds of fences work for different species. A floppy top on this one discourages climbers.

NOT ALL SMOOTH SAILING

Unfortunately, when there are only a small number of animals in your reintroduced population, things that are not usually a problem—like natural predators—can become a major stumbling block. Three of five numbats (another type of marsupial) released in the area were eaten by birds of prey, and all nine reintroduced woma pythons were killed by mulga snakes, also known as king browns—one of the most venomous snakes in the world.

There are multiple fenced parts to the reserve. These allow researchers to conduct experiments to study the impacts of reintroducing wildlife, figure out how native wildlife interact with exotic species, and come up with strategies to help native species survive outside of the fence. Of course, it's also necessary to check the fence on a regular basis and make sure no damage has occurred. This can happen during storms or, because we are talking about Australia, due to fighting kangaroos!

Where there is little chance of removing exotic species, fencing might protect native wildlife. In Australia's deserts, this technique is helping save a lot of marsupials.

BURROWING BETTONGS

GREATER STICK-NEST RATS

THE ARISTOCRATIC DEER

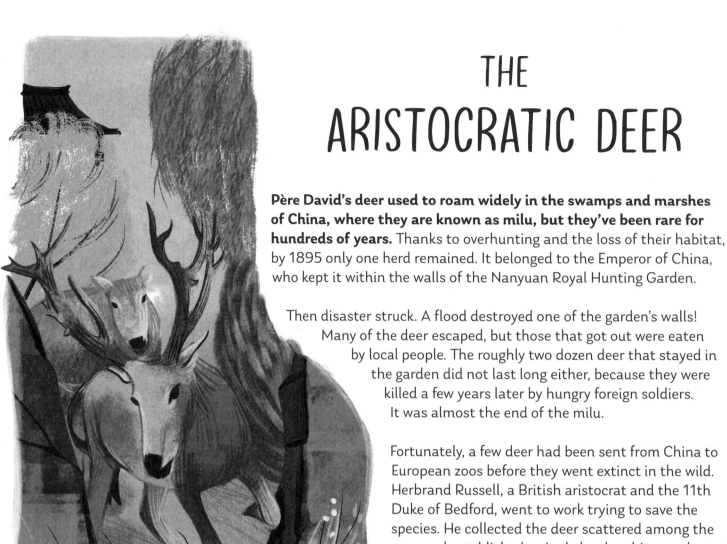

Père David's deer used to roam widely in the swamps and marshes of China, where they are known as milu, but they've been rare for hundreds of years. Thanks to overhunting and the loss of their habitat, by 1895 only one herd remained. It belonged to the Emperor of China, who kept it within the walls of the Nanyuan Royal Hunting Garden.

Then disaster struck. A flood destroyed one of the garden's walls! Many of the deer escaped, but those that got out were eaten by local people. The roughly two dozen deer that stayed in the garden did not last long either, because they were killed a few years later by hungry foreign soldiers. It was almost the end of the milu.

Fortunately, a few deer had been sent from China to European zoos before they went extinct in the wild. Herbrand Russell, a British aristocrat and the 11th Duke of Bedford, went to work trying to save the species. He collected the deer scattered among the zoos and established a single herd on his grand estate in the United Kingdom. The deer seemed to appreciate their new home and began to have babies. Each new birth was good news for the still very rare deer.

RETURN TO CHINA

The first reintroductions to China happened in the 1980s, when a few dozen deer were released south of Beijing. Many other rewilding projects followed, and now there are thousands of Père David's deer roaming through China within dozens of separate herds.

But have they truly returned? Some scientists say no—at least not until new wild herds can be formed and studied for long enough to figure out whether they still need our help to survive. Still, thanks to the Duke of Bedford they have a chance.

THIS UNUSUAL DEER CAN SWIM WELL THANKS TO WEBBED TOES!

Père David's deer only exist today because a few had babies on an English duke's estate around 100 years ago.

CRITICISMS

One major criticism of rewilding projects is that they sometimes fail—even though they take a lot of time and cost a great deal of money. These failures might be because the plants and animals do not make enough babies, or they don't end up surviving long enough to form a population that can exist without our help. To answer this argument, many scientists say that with enough planning and preparation, there is a reasonable chance that a rewilding project can succeed. And we'll never know if we don't try!

TOO CLOSE FOR COMFORT

Another criticism of rewilding projects is that they don't always prioritize the opinions of the people that will be living alongside the reintroduced species. When we are talking about predators like bears or big cats, more wildlife can mean a bigger risk for the people, livestock, and pets that live near them. Some opponents argue that in these cases we shouldn't place a higher value on wildlife than we do on people.

BAND-AID OR CURE?

Some people see wildlife reintroductions as more of a temporary fix than a cure. They might help some wildlife populations, but they do not fix the major problems that caused the species to disappear in the first place, such as hunting or habitat loss. But most scientists would tell you that rewilding projects are not meant to be the solution to all our problems—they are one tool that can help reverse the environmental issues of our past. And rewilding is not meant to replace traditional conservation, but to complement it.

THE TAKE-HOME MESSAGE

Conservation projects should only happen after a lot of thought has gone into doing them right. Rewilding is not always the appropriate answer to a conservation problem, and reintroduction efforts should always be made carefully. It's important local people are involved in the process to reduce conflict between them and any reintroduced species.

THE TIGERS OF SARISKA

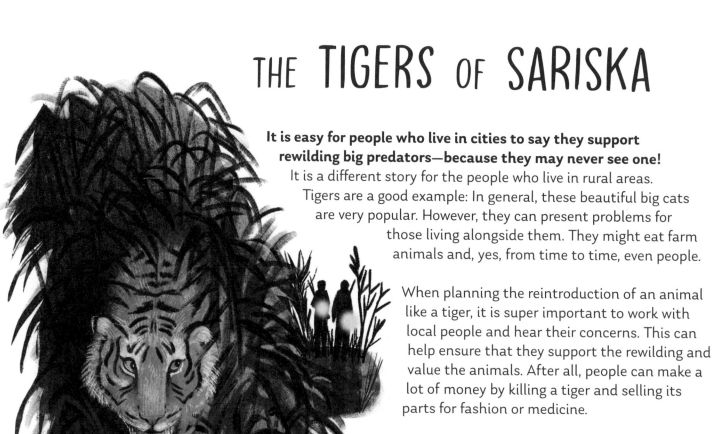

It is easy for people who live in cities to say they support rewilding big predators—because they may never see one!
It is a different story for the people who live in rural areas. Tigers are a good example: In general, these beautiful big cats are very popular. However, they can present problems for those living alongside them. They might eat farm animals and, yes, from time to time, even people.

When planning the reintroduction of an animal like a tiger, it is super important to work with local people and hear their concerns. This can help ensure that they support the rewilding and value the animals. After all, people can make a lot of money by killing a tiger and selling its parts for fashion or medicine.

The poaching of tigers had been a major problem in Sariska Tiger Reserve in India. By 2005 there were no tigers left within its borders. But with this sad story came an opportunity...

A FATHER'S LOVE

About 90 miles (145 km) south of Sariska Tiger Reserve, a female tiger died in Ranthambore National Park. This would have been sad enough by itself, but there was worse news—she had two cubs. Usually tigers are raised solely by their mothers, so these two female cubs were left with little chance of survival. But then something amazing and unexpected happened. Their father appeared! And to the surprise of the local scientists he began protecting his daughters, as well as teaching them how to survive and hunt.

A NEW START

A few other tigers were captured in Ranthambore National Park and moved to the Sariska Tiger Reserve. They made themselves at home, eating everything from monkeys to deer (and livestock too). But one of the males died from poisoning and few new cubs were born. In 2013, the two sisters, now adults, were brought to the reserve. Fortunately, the lessons they had learned from their father helped them thrive in their new home. Both produced cubs of their own, and after a few more years of reintroductions, the population began to grow. There are now thought to be nearly two dozen tigers prowling through the reserve.

A ROCKET THROUGH THE SKY

The peregrine falcon is the fastest animal in the world, capable of reaching speeds of up to 186 miles per hour (300 km per hour). Its speed allows it to surprise its prey, usually other birds, by dive-bombing them before they even notice they're in danger. Although peregrine falcons are impressive predators that are feared by many other species, they were nearly wiped out by chemicals, called DDT, which were used by farmers to kill insects. The problem with spraying these chemicals over an area is that it affects not just the insects, but the plants and anything that eats the insects, too. It affects the whole ecosystem! Eventually it reaches predators. For many birds of prey, DDT changed how the birds made their eggs, and the shells became too thin for the babies to survive. Populations were decimated. In the United States, peregrines were put on the endangered species list in 1970, and DDT was banned not long after that. The stage was set to bring back the majestic hunter of the skies.

DDT was a popular pesticide in the mid-20th century. It was sprayed on farm crops to kill insect pests.

INDEPENDENT CHICKS

First, researchers learned how to successfully breed falcons and raise chicks without them getting too attached to humans. The chicks were placed in boxes high off the ground. Food was dropped in through a small opening, without the birds seeing humans or associating them with food. When the chicks were old enough to start flying, the box was opened and less food was provided, encouraging the young birds to find their own. This strategy was a huge success. By 1999 the species was removed from the endangered species list! Similar projects helped these awesome creatures to recover in other countries around the world.

URBAN BIRDS

Interestingly, this bird of prey, which was once nearly extinct, is comfortable not only in wild and isolated areas, but in cities too. Some peregrine falcons nest on window ledges and churches, others on bridges. They all benefit from lots of pigeons to eat. Some cities set up live cameras on urban falcon nests, so you can watch these birds raise their young on your computer. The next time you're in a city, look up—you might be surprised by what you see!

SOME PEREGRINE FALCONS MIGRATE MORE THAN 6,000 MILES (10,000 KM) EACH YEAR.

41

THE SNOT OTTERS

Hellbenders are some of the largest amphibians in the world, and they have some of the most interesting names too. They're also known as snot otters, due to their slimy skin, and lasagna sides, because of how their skin folds up alongside their bodies. Not everyone believes they are pretty, but they sure are popular, with many passionate supporters.

Hellbenders are completely aquatic salamanders. They live within clear mountain streams through much of the eastern and central United States. But the snot otters are very sensitive to water quality, and their populations suffer badly if there is a lot of pollution or erosion. When trees are removed from the riverbanks, there are fewer roots to keep silt and dirt from entering the water, and this debris covers up the rocks that hellbenders use to hide and raise their young.

Sometimes you might not know that a hellbender population is in trouble until it is too late! Adults can live for a long time, giving the impression that everything is fine, but in the meantime, they are not producing babies. Eventually the old salamanders disappear, leaving an empty stream.

Several zoos have played an important role in developing captive breeding strategies for both the Ozark hellbender and the Eastern hellbender. Sometimes this involved creating large artificial stream habitats complete with flowing water. To the delight of the hellbender supporters, the scientists cracked the code! These facilities have produced thousands of babies that have eventually been released back into the wild.

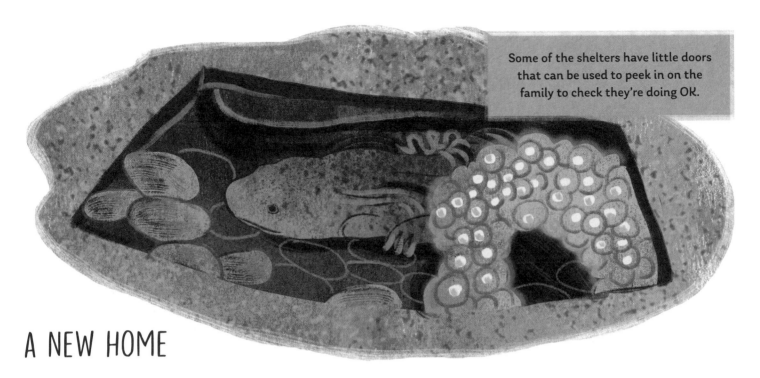

Some of the shelters have little doors that can be used to peek in on the family to check they're doing OK.

A NEW HOME

In addition to the releases, biologists have been helping hellbenders in the wild by placing artificial rock shelters in the streams. These are safe places where the amphibians can raise their babies.

There has been much encouraging news surrounding hellbender reintroductions. However, releases and human-made dens will have little long-term impact on the rare salamanders unless we also tackle the larger problems still dirtying up hellbender streams.

BEWARE OF THE TOAD!

Quolls are a group of predatory marsupials living in Australia and New Guinea, the largest of which get about the size of a big house cat. Northern quolls are one of the smaller species. They are found along the coastal areas of northern Australia. And they're in big trouble—thanks to a not-so-tasty toad.

Cane toads are not originally from Australia. They were released in the first half of the 20th century to help gobble up some beetles that were eating sugar cane, an important crop for farmers.

Unfortunately, the cane toads *really* liked it in Australia. They exploded in numbers, and while they had little effect on the beetles, they impacted other native wildlife tremendously. Cane toads are poisonous, and any predator that tries to eat them can die. Because Australia's native wildlife were unfamiliar with the toads, many predators were poisoned, including northern quolls.

Biologists wanted to reintroduce northern quolls, but there were still millions of cane toads around and no real hope of getting rid of them. What to do? Well, they tried to teach captive quolls to avoid cane toads by feeding them small toads (which weren't as dangerous) laced with chemicals. The chemicals made the marsupials sick but didn't kill them.

The northern quoll is known by indigenous groups as *njanmak, djabo, bangajii,* or *wijingarri.*

Over time, the quolls learned that cane toads should be avoided. Amazingly, quolls released into the wild often remembered their training and stayed alive, even while surrounded by toads.

TOAD SAUSAGES

The creative work done by biologists to train quolls has seen great success, but there are still important questions to answer. For example, how do we teach wild quolls to avoid toads? It is not known whether mother quolls will pass on the knowledge they have gained to their offspring. One interesting potential solution has been tried: Researchers in helicopters have dropped lightly poisoned toad sausages into the wilds of Australia. They hope that the marsupials get just sick enough to learn not to mess with cane toads. Will it work? Time will tell.

SURROUNDED BY PLANTS

Although animals get a lot of attention, it is important to appreciate plants too! Look out of the window or take a walk, and count how many plants you see. Keep track of how many different *kinds* of plants you see as well. You'll quickly understand how many are all around us, and you'll notice all their different shapes and sizes too. When a plant goes extinct in the wild, we should consider rewilding it for the same reasons we reintroduce animals—because each species is unique and special, and they have important roles to play in the wider ecosystem.

PLANTS AND TREES ABSORB CARBON DIOXIDE...

CARBON CAPTURE

Plants are good for us. Through a process called photosynthesis, they absorb a gas called carbon dioxide from the atmosphere, which they store in their leaves, stems, and trunks. In return they release the oxygen we need to breathe. This means without plants we would all die! Excess carbon dioxide, produced by burning fuels like oil and coal, is one of the main reasons for climate change. Just imagine how much carbon must be stored in a forest!

...AND RELEASE OXYGEN.

TREE HOUSE

Plants are important for other species, too. Trees provide important homes, hiding spots, and food for wildlife. Picture a massive fig tree from Central America. Snakes hide within the branches. Monkeys stay safe from predators like jaguars, while parrots eat the fruit. Some of the fruit falls to the ground, where it is eaten by large plant-eaters like tapirs.

SCIENTISTS HAVE DISCOVERED ABOUT 400,000 DIFFERENT SPECIES OF PLANTS.

THORNY FORTRESS

The saguaro cactus might not look like somewhere *you* would want to live, but this spiky tower block is important to many animals. Gila woodpeckers like to nest within the cactus. They hammer away to create holes, which are later used by many other species, such as owls.

THE MEAT-EATING PLANT

Peat has been harvested from boggy wetlands for hundreds of years.

Plants need sunlight and water. But if you have ever tried to take care of a houseplant, you'll know it can be a lot more complicated than that! Some species need a very specific combination of the two things. Plants also need nutrients. We get our nutrients from the food we eat. Most plants get their nutrients through photosynthesis and from the soil. Not all soil is the same—and some soil doesn't contain many nutrients at all. Bogs often have soil that is low in nutrients. So what do you think some plants that grow in boggy habitats have evolved to do? They started eating meat! These carnivorous plants trap and digest insects, spiders, and sometimes even small creatures like frogs. They get their nutrients from animals instead of the soil.

A PLANT IN DANGER

Venus flytraps may be the best-known carnivorous plants, but there are also many called sundews. Sundews use a different strategy to catch their prey: They have sticky tentacles that attract and trap bugs. One species in particular, the great sundew, became very rare in the United Kingdom. Its boggy habitats were rich in something called peat, which was harvested by humans to be used as fuel. Botanists (that's the name for people who study plants) knew that something had to be done.

SOWING THE SEED

By taking cuttings of wild plants, botanists could grow new plants in captivity, feeding them little bits of insects by placing them on their sticky tentacles. As bogs begin to be restored in the UK, scientists now have the plants to bring back, too. And unlike many animals, just a few plants can produce thousands of seeds, allowing them to spread across their former habitats fairly quickly. Many people are now eagerly waiting for sundews to be a common sight in the UK once again. The insects... not so much.

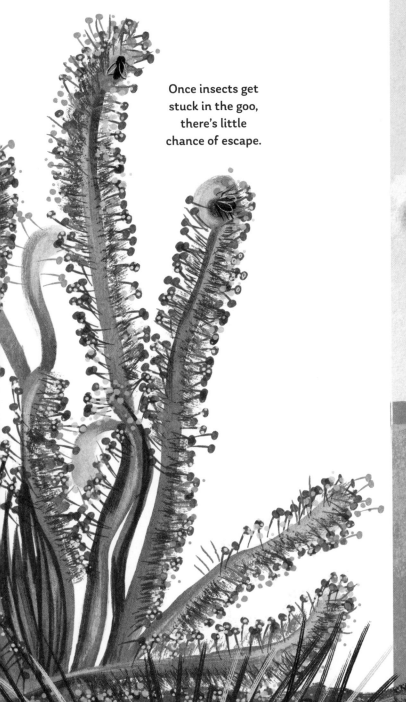

Once insects get stuck in the goo, there's little chance of escape.

WHAT IS PEAT?

Peat is a special kind of soil that is usually found in wetlands, like bogs. It is made mostly of plants that have not completely broken down, or decomposed. The largest peat bog is in Russia and it is huge—bigger than most countries in Europe! Peat has a variety of uses but is probably best known for its use in gardening soil (you should always try to buy peat-free soil). Sometimes peat is taken from bogs, and sometimes the bogs are drained so people can grow crops or trees. In either case, the peat bogs are damaged. It takes thousands of years to develop thick layers of peat, but they can disappear in an instant.

For a peat bog to form, it has to rain—a lot.

Dead plant material from the forest above starts to compact in layers. A waterlogged dome is created.

Peat, like plants and trees, acts as a carbon store. The more peat bogs the world has, the more carbon is taken out of the atmosphere. If we want to protect the planet from climate change, we need to protect peat bogs.

THE LYNX EFFECT

There was once a species of big cat freely prowling through the forests and grasslands of Portugal and Spain. Today however, the Iberian lynx is one of the rarest cats in the world. The fate of these cats is closely tied to that of rabbits. Adult lynx usually need to catch and eat a rabbit every single day. This means that when things are going well for the rabbits, things are going well for the lynx—but unfortunately the opposite is also true.

Rabbit populations sometimes change dramatically due to diseases, and when there are few rabbits around the lynx populations shrink. Thanks to the lack of rabbits, plus car collisions and habitat loss, by the early 2000s there were probably fewer than 100 wild Iberian lynx left. A group of organizations joined forces and got to work. A captive breeding program produced cubs, which were released into the wild. It is now thought that there are nearly 1,000 wild lynx between the two countries!

THE FUTURE'S BRIGHT

Things are looking very promising for the Iberian lynx. Many are surviving, making babies, and expanding their range. Interestingly, the lynx sometimes eat the foxes that prey on sheep in the region, which has given them an unlikely ally: sheep farmers! But it's not yet time to proclaim victory. It's important to keep monitoring rabbit populations and find out how to reduce their diseases, because the more rabbits there are, the better chance the lynx will have of surviving. Cars remain a big problem too: Many cats are still killed on roads as they move around their territories. All wildlife need space to roam, and that space is sometimes in short supply.

Many of the lynx were released with radio collars, allowing scientists to track them.

THE WILD HORSES

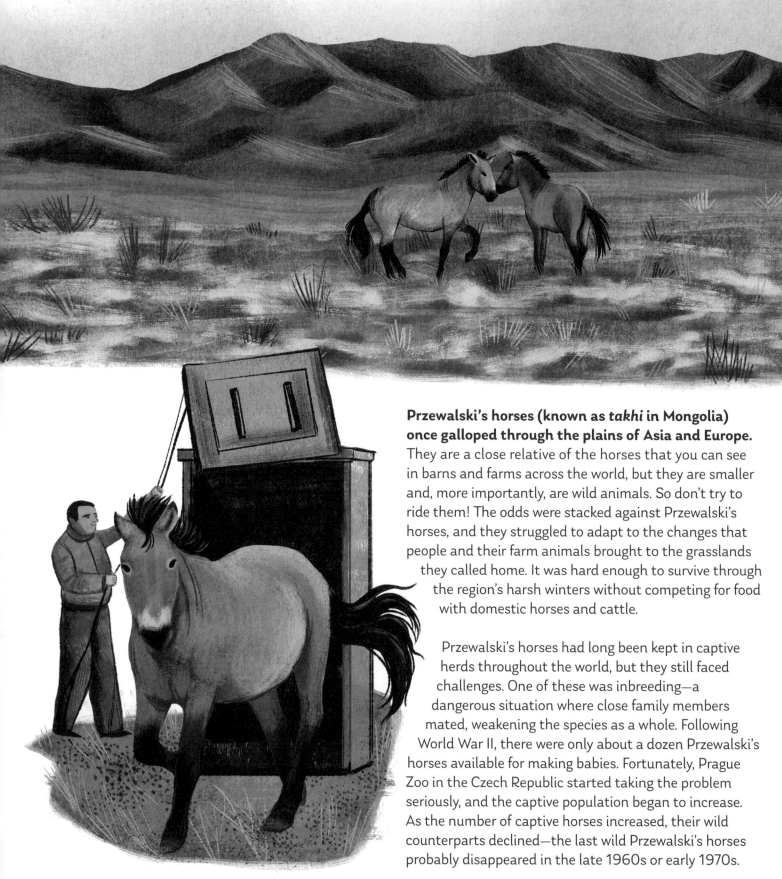

Przewalski's horses (known as *takhi* in Mongolia) once galloped through the plains of Asia and Europe. They are a close relative of the horses that you can see in barns and farms across the world, but they are smaller and, more importantly, are wild animals. So don't try to ride them! The odds were stacked against Przewalski's horses, and they struggled to adapt to the changes that people and their farm animals brought to the grasslands they called home. It was hard enough to survive through the region's harsh winters without competing for food with domestic horses and cattle.

Przewalski's horses had long been kept in captive herds throughout the world, but they still faced challenges. One of these was inbreeding—a dangerous situation where close family members mated, weakening the species as a whole. Following World War II, there were only about a dozen Przewalski's horses available for making babies. Fortunately, Prague Zoo in the Czech Republic started taking the problem seriously, and the captive population began to increase. As the number of captive horses increased, their wild counterparts declined—the last wild Przewalski's horses probably disappeared in the late 1960s or early 1970s.

GIDDYUP

From just a dozen captive horses, eventually there were hundreds—more than enough to start reintroducing them to Mongolia and China, and eventually Russia and Kazakhstan, too. The horses have faced setbacks and have to stay vigilant against predators like wolves, but they seem to be thriving. In addition to those released, many horses also live semi-wild lives in special reserves in Europe.

To keep track of some of the horses released in China, the Chinese government teamed up with the Smithsonian's National Zoo to attach radio collars to the horses. However, there was a problem—the stallions (male horses) didn't like the collars and sometimes destroyed the equipment! So the scientists had to come up with something that wouldn't annoy the horses. One promising idea involved braiding solar-powered transmitters into their tails, which they do not seem to mind. How fashionable!

The horses seem to prefer the trackers in their tails.

53

MEASURING
SUCCESS

What do you think is the most common question that biologists get asked after beginning a wildlife reintroduction? It's probably, "How is it going?" And it's a good question! Biologists also want to know what happens after a rewilding project occurs, and this step is called monitoring. In some cases, monitoring reveals that things aren't going well, and something needs to change. Biologists can monitor individual animals—for example, by attaching radio transmitters to them—or they can monitor the overall population by looking for the animals and then using math to estimate how many there are in the wild. They can also study the effects of the reintroduction on the wider ecosystem by looking at how non-reintroduced species are doing.

RED KITES

In 1990, about a dozen red kites from Spain were released in the United Kingdom, where there were just a handful left hanging on. Today, there are thousands of these birds of prey, making it a very successful rewilding project. But how do we know how many there are? The release is only the first step—in the early years of the project, it was necessary to observe birds and count nests. When dead kites were found, vets rushed to learn the cause of death. Monitoring like this can tell us how reintroductions are going and help identify potential problems.

SEA EAGLES

The last sea eagle was killed in Scotland over 100 years ago. But reintroductions in the 1970s and 1980s returned the bird to the west of the country. More recently, chicks have been released in the south of England, where they hadn't been seen for even longer. All of the birds were released with satellite tracking devices on their backs, which allow scientists to monitor where they fly. Colorful bands on their legs help people on the ground easily recognize the birds.

IN FOR THE LONG HAUL

Monitoring is important to figure out whether a rewilding project is on the path to success. Given all the planning that goes into reintroducing wildlife, success could simply mean releasing the animals. But the job isn't really over then. For a reintroduction to be truly successful, the species should stick around for many years and generations. In the meantime, biologists can look for signs of success, like evidence that the animals are mating and having babies. Often we don't know for many years whether a project is truly successful.

Radio transmitters can track where animals go.

THE MISSING CARIBOU

Reindeer—or caribou, to give them their North American name—used to be a big deal in Maine. There's even a town named after them! But today you won't find any caribou in the state, despite two different rewilding attempts. Too many were hunted for food in the 1800s, a period when they were so popular they were even shipped to other states. At the same time, loggers cut down the old forests they called home and where they found their favorite food: lichen that grows on the bark of trees. It was all too much for the caribou, and they vanished. The people of Maine missed them, and in 1963 two dozen caribou were captured in Newfoundland, Canada, and brought back to the state. Unfortunately, however, within a few years all of them either left the area or died.

CARIBOU AIR

More than 20 years later, scientists decided to try again. They moved caribou by land, air, and sea to Maine with the intention of starting a captive breeding colony. Hopes were high. In 1989, 12 of the caribou produced from this herd were released, but most were dead within a year... Although the released caribou had four calves, all these animals died as well. The sad news kept piling up—why did the reintroductions keep failing?

NATURAL PREDATORS

Overhunting and overlogging are probably the main reasons why caribou went missing from Maine in the early 1900s, but natural predators like black bears, bobcats, and coyotes helped doom the reintroductions. To these carnivores it was like a waiter had just served dinner on a big silver plate! If there were lots of caribou around, these predators wouldn't have a big impact, but when there are so few animals in the first place, each individual is very important. If the caribou are ever to return to Maine, different tactics must be used.

SAVING THE STURGEON

Baby sturgeon are called fry.

When you think of a fancy restaurant, you might think of waiters serving champagne and caviar— but do you know where caviar comes from?
Sturgeon are a group of fish that haven't changed much for millions of years. Some can get big, well over 10 ft (3 m) long, although most are smaller. In general, sturgeon tend to live in saltwater habitats, but they swim upstream into freshwater rivers to spawn and lay eggs.

DANGEROUS DELICACY

Caviar

It's their eggs that caused them trouble. You guessed it—caviar. Unfortunately for sturgeon, their eggs are a very popular delicacy around the world. As a result, too many sturgeon were harvested for their eggs, removing the big old females that are most important to the population. Along with dam building and declines in habitat quality, this has caused most sturgeon to be very rare today. Some are already extinct.

In Europe, the beluga sturgeon has been the focus of rewilding efforts in countries including Hungary, Bulgaria, Romania, Austria, and Germany. Young sturgeon, called fry, are raised in artificial streams until they are a few months old. Then they are released into the Danube River, which was historically home to six different species of sturgeon. Biologists aren't resting though—illegal fishing for sturgeon remains an important issue that needs addressing. But conservation efforts will help ensure the species sticks around in the meantime.

WHAT IS OVERFISHING?

These days it's rare to catch wild animals from fields and forests to sell as food, but it's not unusual in the ocean. Fishing boats catch tremendous amounts of seafood and sell it to people on shore, who transport it to restaurants and supermarkets. This is called commercial fishing. The oceans may seem endless, but fish aren't infinite. Due to gigantic trawlers constantly fishing the same areas numerous species have been overfished, and their populations have crashed.

COMMERCIAL FISHING

Commercial fishing can put a lot of pressure on fish populations, and it is difficult to set laws protecting fish because the oceans are so big and they're controlled by lots of different countries. Because of these various complications, it is sometimes a challenge to know if too many fish are being removed from the water.

SUSTAINABLE FISH

It's always important to think before you buy fish. Where did the fish come from? Is it a species in trouble? In general, sustainable seafood tends to be from small and abundant fish, like sardines and anchovies, whereas big creatures like sharks and swordfish are more at risk. It's also important to make sure you're not purchasing from companies that treat their workers poorly. Even today, some companies use slaves to catch fish.

THE JAGUARS OF THE WETLANDS

When you think of jaguars, you probably think of sleek predators stalking through the Amazon rainforest. But that's not the only place these majestic creatures call home. Historically jaguars have been found throughout South America, up through Central America, and even into the south-western region of the United States.

Big predators need large chunks of land to roam, and those can be tough to find these days. And that's not all—jaguars often come into conflict with ranchers concerned about their livestock. They also need to avoid hunters who want to sell their fur. It's no surprise these animals have been wiped out from many of their previous habitats, but a group of people in Argentina in South America are trying to bring them back to Iberá National Park, where they once thrived.

Jaguars are the biggest cats in the Americas, and historically they haven't gotten along well with ranchers.

TALKING TO THE LOCALS

Doug Tompkins was an active conservationist. Working alongside conservation organizations and government agencies, he started the efforts to rewild Argentina's vast wetlands and savannahs with jaguars. But if hunting was why jaguars disappeared, biologists needed to make sure history would not repeat itself. Doug realized early on that talking to the local people was important. They discussed the plans for releasing the jaguars, which would begin with putting them in cages so they could acclimatize to the area. After lots of meetings, most of the ranchers agreed bringing jaguars back to the wetlands was a good idea, partly because they could bring tourists (and their money) to the region.

THE FIRST CUBS

Because wild and healthy jaguars are hard to come by, biologists decided to focus on producing cubs from cats that were already in captivity, then training them for a life in the wild. They also decided that injured cats they were looking after could be part of the project—especially if releasing them back to where they came from was too risky.

In 2018, the first two cubs in the program were born. And then in 2021, 70 years after jaguars disappeared from the region, three cats were reintroduced to the wetlands! Time will tell if their release will be a success. The organizations involved with the release are focusing on releasing females first, since any males might simply leave to look for mates. The scientists hope the region could eventually support up to 100 jaguars, alongside several other recently reintroduced species including orphaned giant anteaters, pampas deer, tapirs, peccaries, and macaws.

THE ISLAND FOXES

Off the coast of California are a group of islands known as the Channel Islands, some of which contain a special type of fox. Although these island foxes are closely related to the gray fox that lives on the mainland, they have been by themselves long enough that they have evolved into something different and unique.

In the late 1990s, however, it became clear there was a big problem. The foxes on several islands started disappearing—and rapidly. Some of the foxes became sick with canine distemper, a disease that may have come to the islands through raccoons. But there was also a more complicated relationship at play...

Bald eagles are big and territorial. They don't like golden eagles being around.

BATTLE OF THE EAGLES

To explain, we have to shift our attention to eagles. In the 20th century, bald eagles suffered from the wide use of pesticides like DDT, just as peregrine falcons did (see pages 40–41). Their populations started to shrink in alarming numbers. Once they were gone from the islands, golden eagles moved in. Many years ago people had introduced pigs to the islands, and the golden eagles were able to rely on the pigs as a good food source. But that's not all they munched on. While bald eagles had left the island foxes alone, golden eagles ate too many of them!

To help the island foxes, biologists had to first help the ecosystem. This meant removing pigs, relocating the golden eagles to other areas, and bringing back bald eagles—who, sure enough, kept the golden eagles from returning.

The islands became comfortable and safe again for foxes, and biologists released more animals raised in a captive breeding program. Overall, the project was a great success, and there are now thousands of wild island foxes once again enjoying that Pacific Ocean breeze.

Farm pigs were brought to the islands in the 1850s. Eventually some escaped and attracted golden eagles.

PLEISTOCENE REWILDING

By now you know that reintroducing an animal is not always just about helping that one particular species. It is also about helping the ecosystem. Well, what happens when a species is extinct, there are no animals in captivity, and rewilding is not an option? Some scientists have proposed a controversial strategy: introducing an animal that is similar to the extinct species and can fill the same role. Perhaps there is no such plan more controversial than Pleistocene rewilding. Most reintroduction efforts focus on species that have gone extinct in the last few hundred years. But supporters of Pleistocene rewilding say that humans started hunting species to extinction much earlier than that—thousands of years ago in fact, during a time known as the Pleistocene.

THE LAST CAVE
LION PROBABLY WENT
EXTINCT AROUND
11,000 YEARS AGO.

PLEISTOCENE PARK

In Russia, there is an ambitious project underway to restore the ancient grasslands of the far north. It's called Pleistocene Park. To keep the area open and free from trees, big herbivores are needed to munch on the vegetation—animals like bison, reindeer, wild horses, and musk ox. These creatures can be seen browsing there now, but a big piece of the puzzle is still missing: mammoths. Mammoths are extinct of course, but the owners of Pleistocene Park are hoping that new technologies, like cloning, will soon bring them back to life.

Why are North American pronghorn antelope among the fastest land animals in the world? Perhaps because they used to have to outrun cheetahs, who once lived in North America!

UNUSUAL SIGHTS

In North America, some scientists have proposed introducing species like camels, cheetahs, lions, and even elephants. Obviously, it would be pretty shocking to have cheetahs wandering around Kansas, so the plan doesn't have many supporters yet. But all new ideas seem pretty outrageous when they are first proposed!

THE EMPEROR OF THE FOREST

Eastern indigo snakes are one of North America's most impressive snakes. In fact, their Latin name means "emperor of the forest." Glossy black and blue scales glisten in the sun as these reptiles cruise around the longleaf pine forests they call home. Unfortunately the forests started disappearing as humans cut down trees to make room for towns, streets, and crops. There was also another problem: Lightning strikes would start fires in the forests. Sounds bad, right? Actually, these fires helped keep invasive hardwood trees out. Under human management, fewer fires and more hardwood trees were bad news for the indigo snakes' favorite habitat, and their numbers declined.

There was surging interest in restoring the longleaf pine forests and bringing back the snakes that should be living in them. The first step was to catch wild snakes in Georgia that were about to lay eggs, then let them do so in captivity. Afterward, the moms were released back in Georgia. The babies were released in Alabama or allowed to grow up at a special center.

Even people who don't tend to like snakes appreciate indigos because they like to eat venomous snakes, like copperheads.

Indigo snakes, along with hundreds of other species, often live in the burrows created by gopher tortoises, another species in danger.

These snakes eventually started producing babies of their own, which to this day are being released not only in Alabama but also in the Florida panhandle. (The illustration on the right shows me, the author of this book, releasing one of the snakes!)

RETURN OF THE EMPEROR?

At least a few of the snakes are sticking around, finding each other, and breeding. But a successful wildlife reintroduction would be one in which the animals no longer need our help and have enough babies on their own to grow the population. That hasn't happened yet. Some of the snakes have been killed by predators—one was even seen being eaten by an alligator—and others have been run over by cars. And there is still no evidence that the indigo snakes are producing babies that survive long enough to reach adulthood. Many more snakes will be released at both sites. Hopefully the snakes will take it from there, and eventually they won't be such a rare sight in the region.

Reintroduced indigo snakes have been observed eating rattlesnakes, rat snakes, and copperheads, as well as frogs and toads.

THE BIRDS OF GUAM

Guam is a small tropical island in the Pacific Ocean, north of Australia. In the past, Guam's forests were home to around a dozen different species of fascinating birds that could be found nowhere else in the world, but something terrible happened. The Guam kingfisher hasn't existed in the wild for nearly 30 years, and the same can be said for the Guam rail. And they were the lucky ones—because scientists acted quickly to keep some of them alive in captivity. As for the other species, they are considered extinct.

So what happened? Species that evolve on islands are not always used to predators, so they do not need sophisticated defensive strategies. That becomes a big problem when people, who move stuff and animals all over the world, get careless regarding what gets loose. Non-native animals can establish themselves in new areas and start creating problems. Some of the most damaging invasive species on islands are creatures like rats, goats, and rabbits, but on Guam the culprits were snakes.

Guam rails cannot fly. That means they must nest on the ground, where the eggs and young are vulnerable to predators.

A SNAKE IN PARADISE

Brown tree snakes come from Australia, Indonesia, and a few other neighboring islands. In the 1940s, during World War II, there was a lot of military activity in the region. Many boats and planes traveled from island to island, and some of the snakes must have become stowaways, escaping into the forests of Guam.

The birds had never faced a predator like this. The snakes quickly consumed lots of eggs and chicks. Ten of Guam's forest birds were completely eliminated by the snakes, which also decimated lizard and bat populations. Scientists captured 21 rails and 29 kingfishers before it was too late. The Guam rails bred well in captivity and were eventually introduced to a couple of islands near Guam that had not been invaded by snakes. Even though rails are not from these islands, the habitat suits them. Hopefully the Guam kingfishers might join them soon.

You might expect all kingfishers to eat fish, but here's a surprise: This kind prefers insects and lizards!

Scientists are working hard to study brown tree snakes, with the hopes of someday removing them. For now, they're too good at hiding.

THE DISAPPEARING RIVERBANK

Sand is taken from riverbanks to be used in industries such as construction, damaging areas where gharials nest.

Alligators and crocodiles are relatively well known compared to their cousins, the gharials. But gharials have one very distinctive feature that can help you recognize them: their long and narrow snouts. These unique features are helpful for snapping down on the fish they like to eat!

Gharials used to be relatively common in India and a few surrounding countries, but in time they became highly endangered. At first, their problems related to overhunting and getting tangled up in nets and hooks meant for fish and turtles.

Today, however, the biggest threats to gharials are the threats to their river homes. Water is taken for crops, while dams and sand-mining damage the sandbanks where gharials nest and bask in the sun. This can also change the flow of the rivers.

Starting way back in the 1970s, facilities were created throughout India and Nepal to breed captive gharials. Thanks to these programs, thousands of the young reptiles have been released to their historic homes. Some of the first releases occurred on the Chambal River, where gharials had nearly vanished. Today over 1,000 can be found swimming there.

Another rewilding project is ongoing in the Gandak River. Some of the gharials there have radio transmitters attached that will help researchers learn about their behavior. Conservationists are also working hard to protect nests found in the wild from people and predators. There's still work to do, because many of the problems facing Indian rivers have not been completely fixed, but we now know gharials can return if we work hard enough.

Many of the people who rely on healthy rivers, like people who fish, are helping scientists keep track of the recovering gharial populations.

A LITTLE BEETLE LOVE STORY

American burying beetles belong to a group of insects called carrion beetles. "Carrion" means dead flesh, and, you guessed it, these insects love eating dead animals. The males will sniff out the rotting carcass of a small creature and head over to enjoy a tasty meal. Once there, they release chemicals called pheromones that attract females. If multiple males arrive they'll fight first—these dead animals are very precious!

Once a male and female have teamed up, they will bury the carcass. Yhe female will lay eggs close to it. The eggs hatch and the grubs tuck into the carcass, helped by their parents.

Although this species once occurred throughout much of the eastern and central United States, they declined in alarming numbers for unknown reasons. The widespread use of pesticides (them again) may have played a role. Or perhaps these beetles used to feed on dead passenger pigeons. These used to number in the billions before they went extinct, leaving the beetles with little to eat.

Male burying beetles find a dead animal and wait for a female to arrive.

The young beetles (larvae) feed on the dead animal for about a week before they start to develop into adults.

PASSENGER PIGEONS MIGHT HAVE BEEN AN IMPORTANT FOOD SOURCE FOR THE BEETLES.

THE POWER OF LOVE

Scientists decided to try to save the little corpse-guzzlers, but to do so they first had to spark a little romance. A captive breeding colony was started. In it, specific beetles were paired with each other on a flower pot, with a dead quail chick for them to bury together. Then the scientists collected their babies to be used for rewilding projects.

WORK CONTINUES

Numerous states are now working to protect the small beetles where they still occur and reintroduce them elsewhere. In Massachusetts, one reintroduction attempt failed, but another has had better luck. On Nantucket island, biologists released captive-raised beetles. They also trapped wild beetles and put males and females together on small dead creatures. However, it is thought that the beetles are still dependent on human assistance.

Although the reintroduction efforts have resulted in more beetles in the wild, it seems as though there are still some threats that have not gone away. Scientists have noticed there are more medium-sized mammals around now, like raccoons, skunks, and opossums, and they may be eating the dead animals before the beetles can find them. There is a lot of work to be done before we can stop worrying about these amazing creatures.

WHAT CAN YOU DO?

After reading this book, you might be wondering how you can help plants and animals. These pages contain ideas to get you started. It is important to remember that wildlife reintroductions are a last-ditch effort to reverse something bad that has already happened. It is much better and easier to prevent bad things from happening in the first place! To make the world a better home for wildlife, we should think about our personal actions, like reducing the number of things we buy so we don't throw away as much stuff. We should also think about bigger trends in our society, like laws and systems that say making money is more important than caring for the natural world.

EXPLORE YOUR AREA

You could start by learning about the green spaces and natural areas in your neighborhood. Walk around. Make a note of the plants and animals you see, but be careful not to disturb them. To get a sense of who your natural neighbors are, see if the same species appear month after month. If you spot litter, pick it up (but always do so with the help of a parent or guardian and use a trash-picker and glove—you don't want to cut yourself on something sharp).

SHARE YOUR PASSION

One of the most important things you can do for plants and animals is to gently tell other people why you appreciate them. You might end up convincing them to help wildlife too! Making posters is a great way of informing people about the issues you care about. You could even start a campaign to save a particular species.

SAVE OUR TREES

BEES ARE GREAT

HAVE YOUR SAY

Do you know which politicians represent you? Do you know their positions on wildlife conservation? Do they know yours?

It can sometimes feel like politicians exist in a different world, but there are ways you can get their attention. Let your local elected officials know you value wild species and the places where they live. You never know, you might help shape future laws that protect the planet!

MAKE IT WILD

If you have a garden, even a small one, you can help make it a nice place for plants and animals. When gardening, choose to plant native varieties that are from your area. You will have a bunch of plants that feel comfortable without needing a lot of special care, and they can provide shelter and food for a wide variety of insects and birds. Think about whether you can create a small wetland area where animals can visit and drink. And keep cats and dogs away from wild animals!

75

GLOSSARY

Amphibian
A member of the group of animals that includes frogs, toads, salamanders, and caecilians. They usually have slimy skin and spend time in water and on land.

Apex predator
An animal that preys on other species and does not get eaten by anything else.

Botanist
A person that studies plants.

Captive breeding colony
A group of animals (not in the wild) that exists to produce babies, sometimes for rewilding projects.

Carnivore
An animal that mostly eats meat.

Climate change
Long-term shifts in weather patterns. These are caused not only by natural processes but also by human activity, like burning fossil fuels such as coal and oil.

Conservation
The act of protecting plants and animals today and into the future.

Deforestation
The removal of the trees and forests from an area.

Ecosystem
A group of plants and animals that live in the same habitat and interact with one another and the environment.

Ecosystem engineer
A species that has a major effect on its habitat and surroundings.

Evolution
The gradual change of a species over time, usually so it is better able to survive and reproduce.

Extinct
When a living thing no longer exists in the wild or in captivity.

Food web
The relationships between all of the predators, prey, and plants in an area.

Fry
Small baby fish.

Habitat
The places where a plant or animal is usually found.

Herbivore
An animal that mostly eats plants.

Keystone species
A species that plays an important role in the ecosystem, which would drastically change if the species was gone.

Larvae
The immature forms of animals such as insects, before they change and become adults.

Mammal
An animal that has fur or hair and nurses its young with milk.

Marsupial
A type of mammal that has pouches in which it raises its young—for example, a kangaroo.

Native species
A plant or animal found in an area where it has always existed.

Non-native species
A plant or animal found in an area where it did not originally come from. Also known as an exotic species.

Nutrients
The things in food that help plants and animals grow and have babies.

Omnivore
An animal that eats both meat and plants.

Photosynthesis
The process plants use to get their nutrients and energy from the sun.

Predator
An animal or plant that eats animals.

Prey
A plant or animal that is eaten by something else.

Reintroduction
The release of plants or animals back to an area where they used to live but where they can no longer be found.

Rewilding
Giving an ecosystem a chance to become whole again by releasing plants and animals and allowing the landscape to become wild.

INDEX

This has been a
NEON  SQUID
production

To every person restoring and rewilding nature on our one and only planet.

Author: David A. Steen
Illustrator: Chiara Fedele
Consultant: Julia Mata
US Editor: Allison Singer

Neon Squid would like to thank:

Georgina Coles for proofreading and Elizabeth Wise for compiling the index.

Created for St. Martin's Press by Neon Squid
The Stables, 4 Crinan Street, London, N1 9XW

EU representative: Macmillan Publishers Ireland Ltd,
1st Floor, The Liffey Trust Centre, 117–126 Sheriff Street
Upper, Dublin 1, D01 YC43

10 9 8 7 6 5 4 3 2 1

Printed and bound in Guangdong, China
by Leo Paper Products Ltd.

ISBN: 978-1-684-49222-0

Published in July 2022.

www.neonsquidbooks.com